IMAGES OF ENGLAND

ROCKINGHAM FOREST

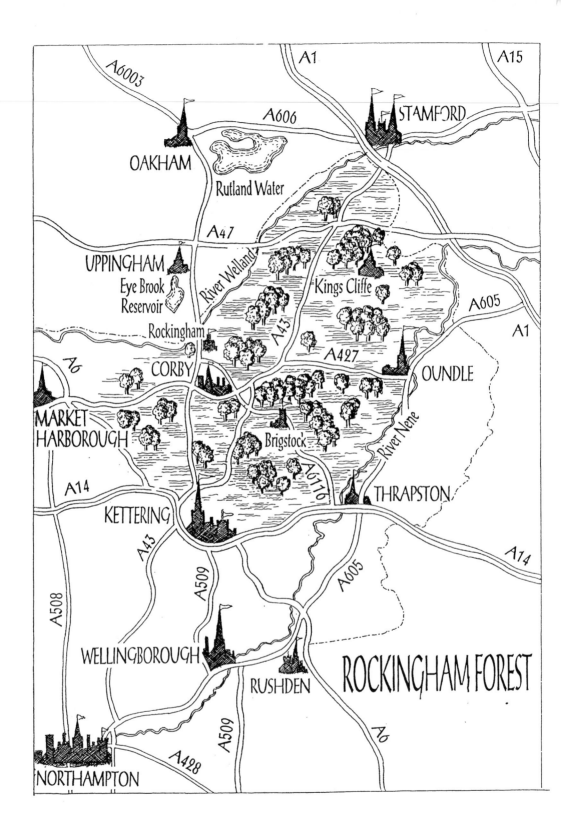

IMAGES OF ENGLAND

ROCKINGHAM FOREST

PETER HILL

TEMPUS

Frontispiece: Rockingham Forest, 2005. The rivers Welland and Nene traditionally form the western and eastern boundaries respectively, with parts of the A14 and A6 now forming the southern end, together with the county boundaries near Stamford and Market Harborough.

First published 2005

Tempus Publishing Limited
The Mill, Brimscombe Port,
Stroud, Gloucestershire, GL5 2QG
www.tempus-publishing.com

British Library Cataloguing in Publication Data.
A catalogue record for this book is available from the British Library.

ISBN 0 7524 3640 6

Typesetting and origination by Tempus Publishing Limited.
Printed in Great Britain.

Contents

Acknowledgements   6

Introduction   7

one   Early Views   9

two   The Forest at Work   21

three   The Forest at Play   49

four   The Forest at War   71

five   Forest Faces   81

six   Forest Places   93

Acknowledgements

I am grateful to the many people past and present who have helped me in getting together the material for this book. Their willingness in temporarily parting with their valued photographs and postcards to share with a wider audience is much appreciated. Their help with this current volume and my previous three books in this series will undoubtedly form a valuable pictorial archive of the Rockingham Forest area for posterity.

The many hours of interviews and shared memories of those who have lived in the Forest all or most of their lives, many of them members of long-established local families who have passed down valuable information, traditions, tales, letters and diaries, have been an enjoyable and edifying experience that has enabled me to set up a detailed, comprehensive database on the region. Some of these villagers who were in the autumn of their lives have since passed on, the last links with a world we have lost, but at least their recollections, which might never have been written down and remained irretrievable, were documented in time.

Among those individuals I wish to thank are Kevin Abrahams, Mabel Adams, Brian Andrews, Cynthia Bagshaw, Irene Beadsworth, Mrs M. Bellamy, Quentin Bland, William Boddington, John Bosworth, Colin Bradshaw, Diane and Barry Bright, Jill Clayton of Easton Parish Council, David and Elizabeth Close, Tony Coales, Mike Crossman, Sarah Downes, Frank Ellis, Myrtle Farmer, Maurice Goodwin and Elvin Royall of the Rothwell Preservation Society, Peter Hall, Jim Harker, Elsie Harrison, Gwen Hay, the late John Hay, Carl Hector, Dr Hibble, Barry Hinton, the late Bob Howe, Judith Hubbard, Annie Johnson, Jill Johnson, Elizabeth Jordan of Gretton Local History Society, Pat Kimmons, Anne Lambert, Jo Langley, David Marsden, Bob Mears, John Measures, Pam Moore, Wendy O' Brien, Chris Owen, Sue Payne and the Willow Brook Local History Group, Toni Palenski, Libby Philips, Harry Pywell, Bill Richardson, Peter Rowney, Mabel Sculthorpe, Evelyn Sharman, Bill and Beryl Simon and Brigstock Local History Group, Audrey Singlehurst, Jane and Peter Smith, Reg Sutton, Alice Thomas and Oundle History Society, Alan Toseland, Sue Trow Smith of Kingscliffe Heritage Archive (with particular thanks to Canon Bryan, Mick Bailey and Mary Bailey), Percy Tyrell, Eileen Watts, the late Stan White, and Iris Wynn. All possible efforts have been made to contact any copyright holders, and apologies are offered if any such ownership has not been acknowledged.

My gratitude also extends to the staff of Corby, Kettering and Oundle Libraries, Northampton Record Office, Oundle Museum, Colin Eaton of the Local Studies Collection at Northampton Library, Rothwell Heritage Centre, the 500th Fighter History Group, Corby Borough Council, English Heritage, and Rockingham Forest Trust who are doing effective and important work in establishing the identity of the area, particularly with the Rockingham Rural Revival project.

Finally, we must be indebted to all those unnamed photographers in the past who have made the effort to record images of life around them, whether for personal reasons or professionally. Thanks to their endeavours, we can get a flavour of how life was, and see long-vanished faces and places from a world that will never return.

Introduction

In medieval times, Northamptonshire was divided into three areas of 'forest': Salcey, Whittlewood, and the largest, Rockingham. The word 'forest' did not mean a large stretch of woodland, but was a legal term for an area chosen for the king and his hunting party, which was placed under a special set of laws to protect trees and certain game (deer and boar). A hierarchy of officials ensured the laws were adhered to by everyone – rich and poor alike – living within these 'royal forests' which had been created around the realm during the reign of William the Conqueror.

Anyone flouting Forest Law – poaching, tree felling and unauthorised land clearance – was subject to a lengthy legal process which, depending on the severity of the crime (and contrary to popular myth), did not lead to mutilation or execution, but the imposition of a fine or a term of imprisonment. Should a miscreant fail to appear before the main Forest Court, the Eyre (which theoretically met every seven years), he would be deemed an outlaw, and there are many recorded cases of this occurring in Rockingham Forest, particularly during the thirteenth century.

Although Forest Law was strict, it did have advantages for those villages living within its jurisdiction, such as unlimited rights of common whereby a community could graze its cattle and certain other beasts more extensively than villages 'outside the Forest', and collect as much *naturally fallen* timber (e.g. from decay, wind or lightning) as they wished, for fuel, repair or other domestic function. This was all subject to certain restrictions and conditions favouring the King's deer, such as winter time when little food was available and the fawning season. The villagers also had to pay a small 'rental' (at a comparatively favourable rate) for grazing rghts, and to ensure their animals were branded with an identification mark.

The disadvantages were also many, however, not least the problem with foresters, who, being unpaid (the only concession being free use of a Forest lodge and refreshment), found devious means of getting some income. There were many complaints from local villages about being forced to buy ale (at above the going rate) brewed by a forester whenever a booth was set up by him for that purpose. Another abuse of the system involved the practice of expedition. Ownership of certain breeds of dog was forbidden, while others had to have three claws removed from their front paws to prevent them from attacking a deer. Some foresters went beyond this and also removed the ball of the foot, charging the owner a small fee in return!

Until 1299, Rockingham Forest spanned the area between the rivers Welland and Nene, and stretched from Stamford in the north, as far as Oxendon Bridge at Northampton, but thereafter slowly shrank as land became 'disafforested' – free from Forest Law – which in turn meant that certain villages now found themselves outside the Forest boundaries. (The map illustrated on the frontispiece shows the current boundaries agreed upon in the 1990s by various organisations, which was used for raising public awareness by placing large brown and white road signs around the periphery, informing travellers that they are now entering 'Rockingham Forest'.)

By the Tudor period, Forest Law had become lax, and apart from a brief period of stringent reinforcement and restoration of the pre-1299 boundaries by Charles I, it had virtually disappeared as landowners managed to purchase large areas of land for their own use, free from control by the Crown (which gladly accepted extra revenue), thereby expanding their estates, nurturing the landscape and creating private woodland which flourished in their hands under careful management and experimentation. Those areas of woodland still in royal hands, however, were not so fortunate. An official report in 1792 declared that royal woods were of no benefit to either the King or the people. Compared with private woodland, they were found to be in a pitiful condition, the result of poor management, lack of skills and motivation, and centuries of constraint and abuse. Eventually, these remnants were placed in the hands of a Commissioner of Woods and Forests, and finally in the care of the fledgling Forestry Commission in 1923.

Crafts and industries developed and flourished using the fine natural resources found in abundance in the area. Initially, charcoal burning was limited because of the large amounts of timber required for iron smelting, both activities being controlled by the Crown who, mindful of the need for woodland protection and seeing the potential for financial gain, employed official 'colliers' to operate in the royal manors of Geddington, Brigstock and Kingscliffe during the medieval era. Forges were set up and operated only under royal grant and patronage. Thus the vast deposits of iron ore, much of which lay close to the surface, which had been worked during the Iron Age, Roman and Saxon periods were never fully exploited until the coming of the railways to the area in the 1870s, heralding the beginning of an important 'new' industry that was to transform the landscape around much of the Forest area, culminating with the construction of one of the largest iron and steel making complexes in the world at Corby, in the 1930s.

The golden-brown or honeycomb-coloured ironstone itself proved to be a valuable building resource and is a common feature of many of the older houses in the Forest. This contrasts with the more durable and expensive creamy or grey limestone found in the Weldon, Wakerley and Kingscliffe areas, which was highly prized and used, not just for many churches and the homes of the more affluent, but for prestigious buildings elsewhere in England, such as the old St Paul's Cathedral in London and the chapel of King's College in Cambridge. A fissile form of limestone quarried in the Collyweston area ('slates') was also celebrated as a valuable roofing material for many years.

Other industries flourished for a long period, notably the medieval pottery industries at Stanion and in the Lyveden area, the products of which found their way to other parts of the Midlands and beyond. Weaving was predominant during the seventeenth and eighteenth centuries, woodturning at Kingscliffe (c. 1690 – c. 1910), and large-scale shoe manufacture in the Kettering district from 1776 until its decline in the latter half of the twentieth century.

Today, the fifty-eight villages that constitute Rockingham Forest still manage to maintain a unique spirit and sense of timelessness. In some cases, a close-knit community spirit still survives, as do many of the older cottages and buildings. Although the same state of preservation cannot be said for the towns, which like elsewhere around the country, are experiencing inevitable and unprecedented growth, they do have an important part to play, providing greater employment prospects and a wider range of leisure activities for an increasing population, and acting as a base for visitors wishing to explore the area with its many attractions.

As the twenty-first century progresses, the future looks bright for Rockingham Forest, as more and more residents, individually, or in groups with specific interests, help it to survive and thrive. They are supplemented by organisations such as Rockingham Forest Trust, Wadenhoe Trust, Rothwell Preservation Society, Oundle Museum, the Wildlife Trust, Woodland Trust and the Forestry Commission (which has its regional headquarters in Fineshade Woods). The 'acorns' being planted today will produce a bountiful heritage for other generations to enjoy tomorrow.

This book, like its three predecessors in this series, takes us back into the area's vibrant past, bringing it alive once again, via images that were meant to be seen, shared and enjoyed – a vanished world frozen in time – our Rockingham Forest heritage.

Dr Peter Hill
July 2005

one

Early Views

Left: A late nineteenth-century etching of the Eleanor Cross at Geddington. Of the thirteen crosses erected to mark the funeral procession resting places of Edward I's wife, en route from Harby in Lincolnshire to London, this is the most perfectly preserved of the surviving three monuments. The old well can be seen to the left of the steps (an inscription 'Built in 1769' is still visible today), and beyond this stands the original building of the Star Inn.

Below: A late nineteenth-century etching of the Market Place, Oundle, as seen from the corner of North Street and St Osyth's Lane. The late sixteenth-century buttercross disappeared, together with some of the neighbouring shops, in 1825, and was replaced with a Market House and Town Hall by Jesse Watts-Russell, using masonry from the redundant church of All Saints at Barnwell.

Fotheringhay, *c.* 1902. One of the most picturesque scenes in Rockingham Forest, the church of St Mary the Virgin and All Saints stands majestically in the background overlooking the river Nene. Only the parish part of the church survives today, the collegiate portion having been demolished during the Dissolution. Some of the rubble was used to build a new bridge over the river in 1573, and this itself was replaced in 1722 by the present four-arch bridge.

An early nineteenth-century etching of the remaining fragment of Fotheringhay Castle. A motte and bailey castle stood on the site in 1100 and was owned, rebuilt and extended in the fourteenth century by the royal York family, one of whom, Richard III, was born there. It was also the place of imprisonment, trial and execution of Mary, Queen of Scots in February 1587. It was demolished in the seventeenth century, the only remaining fragment being part of the bailey; this was resited near the riverside.

The Old Inn, Fotheringhay. This artist's impression from an old engraving shows one of two inns built to accommodate the overflow of guests visiting the castle, during the time of Richard of York and his wife Cecily Neville. The fifteenth-century building shown here was constructed from cornbrash, roofed with Collyweston slates, and stood in Main Street. It was replaced in the eighteenth century by the present building.

The old stone bridge over Harpers Brook at Great Oakley, c. 1901. This area of the village was known as Duckpaddle for its tendency to suffer frequent flooding during heavy rain. The last building in the distance is the village school. Note the rutted road surface in the foreground!

Stanion, *c.* 1902. The group is standing in Main Street, outside a building with former religious connections, possibly a priest's house. The elderly man next to the girls on the right is sitting on the base of a stump belonging to a preaching cross. Today, part of this lies beneath the footpath.

Main Street, Stanion, *c.* 1902. The woman is standing at the gateway of the village poorhouse, now known as Workhouse Row. Tithe Barn Cottage stands at the far end of the street. The long building on the left jutting out towards the street no longer exists.

Left: Blatherwycke Bridge, *c.* 1898. Spanning the Willow Brook, this beautiful bridge of medieval origin has two pedestrian refuges, and several dates inscribed on the parapets when the bridge was repaired, the earliest being 1656. Some of these can be seen in the photograph, accompanied by the initials SOB and the Stafford Knot, a reference to the Stafford-O' Brien family, who were lords of the manor.

Below: Main Street, Wadenhoe, *c.* 1905. The post office seen on the left is said to have been the first rural telegraph office in England, set up by the lord of the manor, George Ward Hunt, who was a member of Disraeli's cabinet, Chancellor of the Exchequer, and subsequently First Lord of the Admiralty. The post office would therefore have played a vital role in keeping close contact with London.

Wadenhoe, *c.* 1904. Home Farm, with its ivy-covered walls, stands on the left. The two thatched cottages standing on the corner of Main Street and Pilton Road, to the right, were demolished after falling down, and today only an open space and gateway mark the site.

Church Street, Wadenhoe, *c.* 1902. The double-fronted thatched building on the left housed the shoemaker, Joe Julyan, and the village shop run by Ellen Julyan, which was noted for providing everything the village housewife needed and more, with a barrel of broken biscuits, sweets and toys, much appreciated by local children! Beyond, on the same side is the King's Head public house. The bottom of the street is a cul-de-sac, from which a track leads up to the church standing on the top of Castle Hill.

Harringworth, *c.* 1930. The cross dates from around 1387 when a market was granted to the Zouch family, lords of the manor at the time. A new head was added in 1850. It stands at the junction with the roads to Wakerley, Gretton, Laxton and Seaton. The open gateway to the old smithy can be seen on the left. Part of the viaduct can be seen in the distance. Spanning the Welland valley, it is one of the longest viaducts in Britain, with eighty-two arches, and 20 million bricks which were reportedly used during its construction from 1875-78.

Two cottages on Gretton Road at Harringworth, *c.* 1929. These were demolished, like other old buildings in the village, in the 1940s. The only survivor from the cottages is the ornate polygonal medieval chimney top (centre), which originally came from the former manor house behind the church. Today it can be seen on the re-roofed nineteenth-century Old Smithy opposite the market cross.

Bridge Street, Brigstock, *c.* 1900, looking towards Park Walk in the distance. The last building on the right is a hostelry, The Fox and Hounds, which was burnt down in 1938.

Corby village, *c.* 1910. The people are standing outside the entrance to Rowlett School in High Street. The school house stands to the left of the gates.

The old bridge over the river Ise between Weekley and Warkton, *c.* 1880. The river acts as a boundary between the two villages, and the bridge has since been replaced by one more suited to the heavier road traffic of the modern era. An arch of an earlier medieval bridge lies under the road. Edward Mutton is standing with a horse on the bridge.

Ashley Road.

Wilbarston, 1890s. An idyllic view of the surrounding landscape from Church Street looking towards Stoke Albany. Brig Lane, an ancient track leading to Ashley, lies at the bottom of the hill to the right. The churchyard is out of view to the left of the boy and child.

Great Oakley Hall, 1858. The hatchment above the porch is that of the recently deceased lord of the manor, Sir Arthur de Capell Brooke, explorer and founder member of the Raleigh Society.

Bottom Bridge, Brigstock, *c.* 1900. The bridge over Harpers Brook is mid-eighteenth century, with a pedestrian refuge. It still exists in Bridge Street, but the river was diverted in the 1950s and a grassy stretch now occupies the area seen in this photograph.

Bulwick, Top Farm, early 1900s. Standing opposite the triangular green, the building has changed little, though the front entrance is no longer in use and is covered in foliage.

Bridge Street, Geddington, *c.* 1895. Seen here shortly before the two buildings on the left were demolished and a Working Men's Club (with an extension added later in 1900–01) erected in their place. The Eleanor Cross stands in the background, and behind it at the top of the hill is one of the old bakeries.

two

The Forest
at Work

Delivering bread and cakes at Rockingham, *c.* 1930. The baker's boy, Reg Goodman, has finished his round and acquired a different kind of goods!

Harvest Time at Weldon, *c.* 1910. A mixed group of people stand behind the reaper, some with guns and hounds who, judging by the number of rabbits displayed, had a successful session as the harvesting progressed.

Right: William Spendlove (1890-1961), member of a Gretton farming family, with a hay cart, *c.* 1933.

Below: Arthur Close and his bread wagon at Duddington, 1930s. His bakery was situated in the main street of Collyweston, part of which is now a village museum.

Above: A group of fellmongers at Jabez Rowell's works in Brigstock, 1920. Fellmongering involved the collection and preparation of hides and fleece from slaughterhouses and butchers, for the leather and woollen industries. The site at Harper's Court is now occupied by sheltered accommodation for the elderly.

Left: Tom Incles, itinerant worker at Weldon. He did a variety of seasonal jobs at Cheyne House in the 1930s, and was always on hand for whatever needed to be done, sleeping on the premises (in the hacking shed).

Haymaking near Geddington Chase, 5 October 1912. This activity usually takes place in early summer, but this particular year had such uncommonly fine weather that another session of haymaking took place in the autumn, after the annual harvest. This magnificent haystack was erected in a field known as Oakley Hills, which was part of Stanion Lodge Farm, worked by F.G. Steward of White Hall, Brigstock, the village where the assembled farmworkers came from. The two horses on the left are Blossom and Khako, and the dog in front of them is Bob. From left to right are: Sam Lettin, John Deans, Harry Humphrey, Joe Starsmore, Jack Wills, Harry Wills, William Starsmore, W. Swan, Jim Beal, David Flecknor, B. Rawson, Harry Blades, Josh Edwards, Robert Deans, G. Bailey, T. Blades, Charles Wright, Brian Hart, G. Palmer, William Lettin and Horace Richardson. The boys in front of them are, from left to right: William Humphrey, Frank Brown, Cecil Flecknor, Jack Steward, Jim Steward and Edgar Denton. Such a large workforce was required, not just because of the size of the meadow, but to ensure that once dry, the hay was stacked as quickly as possible. Carting and stacking was also heavy work, so the more labour the better. The hayloader on the right also helped to make the job easier.

Above: Sheep shearing at Grafton Underwood in the 1920s. From left to right are Frank Henson and Len Walden.

Left: Thatching at Aldwincle, 1991. A considerable number of cottages in the Forest area still have a traditional thatched roof, the demand for which has helped the craft survive and flourish.

Ironstone workers at Sudborough Pits, a quarry near Brigstock, *c.* 1920. The first serious quarrying in the Forest area was by the Islip Iron Co. in 1871, and eventually extended as far as Brigstock. Note the narrow wooden plank (upper left) which was used for transporting ore across the site by wheelbarrow.

An engine with wagonloads of iron ore makes its way along the track from Gretton to Corby, *c.* 1925. Stewarts and Lloyds had been involved in the extraction of iron ore since 1884.

Grafton Underwood, *c.* 1902. The village blacksmith, George Welton Clark, is standing in the doorway of his forge, seen in the background. Note the fine array of wheeled vehicles, among which is a delivery wagon belonging to Kettering grocer and draper, Lewis Lewin, who was one of the local traders regularly supplying the village with various goods. Grafton had two shops at this time, one of which was run by Mary Ann Eady; the other, a bakery, grocer's and post office run by William Pearson. Photography was still something of a novelty and special occasion, arousing a sense of curiosity and enthusiasm in such a peaceful place, with villagers willingly posing for the visiting photographer.

The smithy stood on the church side of the brook, which runs parallel with the road for the length of the village; access across the water was and still is via a series of small bridges dating from the eighteenth and nineteenth centuries.

Opposite above: Ironstone quarrying at Easton on the Hill, 1890s. Although the surrounding area was renowned for its fissile limestone deposits, there were also good quantities of ironstone which were exploited, as seen at this quarry lying between the village and Ketton.

Opposite below: Rockingham Estate workers, *c.* 1930. The men were engaged in all kinds of tasks around the vast 4,000 acre estate, including clearance of the castle moat. From left to right are H. West, H. Jarvis, R. Marlow, and T. Woolley.

Cut and shaped blocks of quarried limestone are being winched and loaded onto horse-drawn wagons at Weldon, in the 1890s. It was (and still is) one of the finest building stones in Britain, its durability evident around the Forest, and elsewhere in the kingdom such as the chapel of King's College, Cambridge, and the original St Paul's Cathedral in London. It is strong testimony to its qualities that so many old buildings have survived, with little or no renovation. Weldon stone is of an even-textured quality with few shells. When quarried it is yellowish in colour and soft in texture, but on drying it hardens and turns shades of grey. It is easily worked and can be cut in any direction, making it a mason's favourite raw material. The blocks of freshly quarried stone were originally transported to their destination by ox cart and river craft. For centuries, Weldon masons, such as those from the Grumbold and Frisby families, were in great demand for their skills. The craft has recently been revived in Weldon itself by limestone masons, for house building.

Opposite above: The Old Smithy, High Street, Gretton, 1970. This was one of three forges flourishing in the village in the 1800s and in the early years of the twentieth century. It was used in the 1880s by William Bradshaw Smith.

Opposite below: Frank Hubbard, blacksmith, at his forge in Collyweston, 1930s. The forge still stands on the road to Stamford, though, like all others, it is no longer in use. Since the 1990s, however, one forge started up again, at East Carlton Park, where visitors can watch the skills of a resident blacksmith once again.

Nassington station, *c.* 1900, with the stationmaster, Mr Randall, standing in the centre of the group. Built in 1879, the station was on the Rugby–Peterborough branch of the London North Western

Opposite

Above left: Forest-area tiler 'Dickie' Liquorish of Wansford displaying his skills, with an innovative method of carrying slates while at work on a local house in the late 1950s.

Above right: A Collyweston slater is seen here in 1930 splitting the slabs with a special tool, traditionally made in the village for that purpose. Another tool was made for dressing the stone.

Below: Collyweston was noted for the fissile form of limestone found in abundance in the area which provided a fine, durable roofing material known as slate. Slabs were laid out on frosty nights and watered constantly, enabling them to be split easily, a stack of which stand to the right. An advertisement for one of Oundle's former shops in Market Place, 1926. Telephones were not a common feature at the time, the post office having telephone number one, and this store having number two!

Railway which passed through the Forest area, via Kingscliffe, Wakerley and Barrowden, and to Rockingham and Caldecot, and beyond. It closed in 1957, and the magnificent Nassington Viaduct which had dominated the surrounding landscape was demolished in 1961.

One of the engines formerly in use by the Nassington and Barrowden Mining Co., which is now used by the Nene Valley Steam Railway for nostalgic pleasure trips to Peterborough. Standing on this particular engine, *Jacks Green* (named after a quarry site between Kingscliffe and Yarwell), is Jimmy Hopkins.

Yarwell Junction signalbox, *c.* 1910. Though the line later closed in the 1960s, the box has since enjoyed a new period of active employment with the Nene Valley Steam Railway.

A navvy hut in Gretton, built for railway workers in the 1870s. It stood in Arnhill Road, and was demolished in 1993. Tradition has it that this particular hut, one of several, was used as an office by the railway contractors.

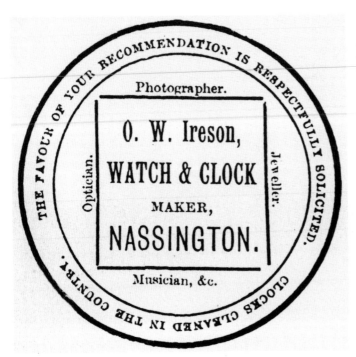

Left: A member of a long-established line of Forest families, Oakley Ireson of Nassington worked extensively around the Willow Brook area as a watch and clock maker, and photographer in the 1890s and early 1900s producing a fine record of the times via high-quality images of faces and places. This trade stamp shows he was also a man of many talents, among them jeweller, optician and musician.

Below: A horse-drawn lawnmower at work in the grounds of Rockingham Castle, 1920s.

Above: The windmill at Brigstock, 1890. Standing to the south of Stanion Road this tower mill was in use throughout the 1800s, but was derelict by 1900. It was one of two windmills in the village, the other being a post mill standing near Geddington Chase. These were two of twenty-seven windmills recorded in the Forest.

Right: Weldon Post Mill, *c.* 1902. It stood in Larratt Road until 1916, when it was blown down in a storm. It was brought from its original site at Wing in Rutland, together with another windmill, in 1839, and ground corn until the end of the century.

Middleton Garage, 1920s. Until recently, a garage stood on the site next to the Red Lion pub on The Hill. At the time it was run by Eric Adams and his brother as a base for a coach and local bus service that had been started by their father, formerly publican at the Woolpack, around the time of the First World War. Two Model T Ford cars, and the rear end of a Commer charabanc (in the doorway), can be seen.

William Bailey turning a powder bowl at the treadle lathe in his workshop at Kingscliffe, 1930s. He was the last in a long line of woodturners that had been working in Kingscliffe since the late seventeenth century, during which time the village became renowned for its 'treen' (wood products). In Victorian and Edwardian times, they would work outside their homes in groups, chopping the wood into billets, shaping them, boring, chiselling and finishing by hand. The types of wood used would depend on the item being made, for example, willow for spoons and bread boards.

Above: A group of woodturning 'students' with their handiwork at Kingscliffe in the 1890s. The vicar of the church, the Revd Du Pre, organised classes for villagers in an old school room in Bridge Street. This was one of the buildings erected by the theologian William Law (1686-1761) for the benefit of the poorer classes of the village.

Right: Kingscliffe Tower Mill. Built in 1818 for William Cunliffe, this fine mill flourished until around 1910 and was reluctantly demolished in 1925. It was unusually positioned, some might say precariously, in the middle of the village, just off West Street. Another windmill stood on the road to Apethorpe, but was demolished around 1860.

Timber haulage at Brigstock, *c.* 1910. A dray ('drug') belonging to the Spencer family of Brigstock is transporting a felled tree in nearby woods. The business had been started in the village in 1868 by Charles Newman Spencer (born 1842 in Stanion) and soon became of great importance in the Forest timber industry, the other main centres of which were at Geddington, Stanion and Kingscliffe (the latter still operating a sawmill).

Tree felling at Deene Park, *c.* 1920. The gang probably worked for Spencer's timber business.

Above: Workmen at Tom Beeby's woodyard, off Park Walk, Brigstock in the 1920s. This was the other woodyard in Brigstock, and stood on the other side of the village from Spencer's yard.

Right: Jim Bass, underkeeper for the Rockingham Castle estate, *c.* 1930.

Rushton Hall, *c.* 1930. Chauffeurs with a Rolls Royce belonging to visitors outside the stable block in the grounds are seen here. The Breitmeyer family were occupiers of the Hall at the time.

Rockingham Fire Brigade, 1930s. Stored by the upper lodge at the top of Rockingham Hill, the engine was never used which may have been fortunate since no water supply was in the vicinity. The group includes the gamekeeper, Sid Masters (centre with the felt hat) and the head gardener, Charles Mears (third from the right).

Brigstock Fire Brigade, April 1944. From left to right, back row: J.E. Bailey, Archie Bell, Jack Bailey, Ernie Bell. Front row: Herbert Newcombe, Jack Allen, Horace Hector.

Perio Mill, in the 1920s. This is the only reminder of the deserted medieval village of Perio that stood close by. The part sixteenth-century watermill originally ground corn until the early eighteenth century when it became a paper mill until around 1852, before reverting to its former use. It is one of several mills that survive on the river Nene, though all have long since ceased functioning.

Brigstock, *c.* 1913. A group of builders and carpenters pose with the tools of their trades. The man holding the plank is Foscuit Wills, one of several villagers who would lose their lives in the First World War.

Grafton Underwood in the 1890s. The group of men are at the church end of the village and are engaged in cleaning out the narrow brook. The luxuriant horse-chestnut trees in the background can still be seen today.

Above: Widening and deepening the river Ise at Geddington, 1953. This was a necessary task because of the river's historical tendency to flood around this area of the village.

Right: Charlie Mears, head gardener at Rockingham Castle, 5 July 1925. He is standing beside a floral cross he has made for the funeral of the Revd Wentworth Watson, holder of the castle.

Girls at work at Wallis and Linnell's clothing factory, Brigstock, 1930s. Frederick Wallis and John Linnell founded a business in Kettering in 1856, and then expanded into the Forest area, setting up factories in Brigstock (1870), Cottingham (1874), and Gretton (1890). The business flourished for many years, reaching international status. The building was known as the Matchbox, because of its tall narrow shape, designed to let in the maximum amount of light for the machinists.

Geddington, *c.* 1900. Mr Clipstone, a worker on the Boughton House estate, is sitting outside the Star Inn, close to the Eleanor Cross. The vast estate gave a lot of employment to several villages in the area.

Archaeological excavations at Priors Hall, between Weldon and Deene, during September 1953 uncovered a large Roman site with bath-house and tessellated pavements. Judging by numerous other Roman sites in the Forest, the area seems to have been a favourite area for occupation, and the exploitation of its fine natural resources.

POST OFFICE EASTON. 103

The old post office in Church Street, Great Easton, 1906. The tower of the church of All Saints is visible in the distance.

Left: Another artefact uncovered during ironstone quarrying was this ornate late Iron Age mirror unearthed west of the church at Desborough in 1908. It is one of the best preserved of its kind, and is now in the British Museum.

Below: This small bronze horse was one of four figurines found with other artefacts at an Iron Age and Romano–British sacred site just outside Brigstock in 1961. The temple complex, with the foundations of polygonal and circular structures, like those discovered at Collyweston in 1953, is unique in Britain.

three

The Forest
at Play

Distribution of the 'Bread and Bun Dole', at Geddington, *c.* 1927. The custom began in the eighteenth century when a Lady Montagu, of nearby Boughton House, decided that all the poor in the village, who normally lived on low-grade rye or barley bread, should enjoy at least one 'white wheaten loaf' a year. On May Day, at the start of the dole, a bell would ring and the bread would be distributed. The custom continues today, with a small piece of bread.

Queen Victoria's Diamond Jubilee celebrations at Rockingham, 1897. The Inchley family stand outside their flag-bedecked cottage. The flower arrangement above the doorway reads: Good Luck.

The custom of decorating bicycles became popular at the time of the coronation of Edward VII in 1902. This photograph was taken around 1910 in the grounds of Geddington Vicarage as part of the annual summer Flower Show, with Eunice Goodman and May Clipstone proudly displaying their handiwork.

Nassington Show, late 1940s. By this time the custom of decorating bicycles had virtually died out, Nassington being the last Forest village to continue the tradition. Displaying their bicycles for a competition are Kenneth Sewter and Valerie Rusdale.

May Day on The Green, Nassington, 1920. The building in the background on the left is Nassington House which at the time was where Stilton cheese was made by the owner, Mr Tyler and his daughter, Katie. In the centre is the schoolmaster's house, and on the right is the school itself, with its distinct cupola dome which was rebuilt in 1894. In the foreground, on the extreme right, is the Nassington Hand Laundry run by a Miss Watson. The May Queen is Annie Ireson, and the man standing on the far left is the headmaster, Mr Howitt.

May Day on the village green, Weldon, c. 1930. The May Queen is Betty Robinson.

Maypole dancing in the grounds of the Latham School, Brigstock, *c.* 1922. The girl on the immediate left is Win Hill, and opposite her on the right is Amy Allen. The boy standing between them in the foreground is Bernard Hector.

May procession, Brigstock, 1950. There had been a long tradition of transporting the May Queen and her retinue around the village by horse and cart. The May Queen here is Ruth Gray and the man leading the horse is Frank Bell.

May Day at Easton on the Hill, 1920s. Decorated bicycles are also in evidence in this parade around the streets. The May Queen, her retinue and the garland are at the back of the procession.

May Day at Grafton Underwood, 1912. The group are posing with a typical traditional Northamptonshire garland, decorated with dolls, foliage and flowers.

May Day at Nassington, 1920, taken in the school grounds. The May Queen is Phyllis Dixon.

'Bringing the Past to Life'. A costumed May procession in Grafton Park Wood, 1996. Organised by Rockingham Forest Trust, the walk included over thirty children from local schools participating in the event.

The Corby Pole Fair at Stocks Lane, May 1902. Two fairs had their origins in the reign of Henry III, when a charter was granted in 1226 to Henry de Braibroc. These were replaced in 1585 when Elizabeth I granted a charter for a fair to her court favourite, Sir Christopher Hatton, lord of the manor, 'for services rendered by the inhabitants of Corby' (supposedly – but inaccurately – for rescuing her from a marsh while she was out hunting). The charter was later reconfirmed by Charles II. Banners and decorated archways were set up at the four entrances to the village, where the charter was read, after which anyone wanting access had to pay a toll for which they were given a ticket as proof of compliance, that some liked to wear in their hats. Any man who refused to pay was carried on a pole, or in the case of a woman, by chair, and placed in a special set of stocks with five holes. Various explanations have been offered as to why there an odd number of holes, including one theory that the extra hole was for one-legged tipplers! Some of the luckier 'miscreants' received a half pint of beer to ease the strain, or endure a period of longevity in the stocks! The pole or stang was also featured in other customs elsewhere, as a means of targetting social disapproval at anyone upsetting community life by straying from the appropiate pattern of behaviour. A costumed pageant, written for the 1922 fair by the rector, T.G. Clarke, was acted by schoolchildren, and included a short play based on the Elizabethan connection with the village and charter, morris dancing and traditional songs such as 'Under the Greenwood Tree'. For reasons that have never been satisfactorily explained, the fair is only held every twenty years, the most recent occasion being 2002; it has always been a fun occasion with additional amusements and activities reflecting the fashion or mood of the times.

Right: The cover of a souvenir programme for the 1947 Pole Fair at Corby. It should have been held in May 1942, but this being at the time of the Second World War, was not possible. With life now more settled, it was decided to hold the fair that year. As well as the traditional features such as the Reading of the Charter, the pageant and placing in the stocks, new attractions appeared such as climbing a greasy pole, racing and a circus.

Below: The Rowell Charter Fair, May 1900. A charter was granted by King John in 1204 to be held the day after Trinity Sunday (now celebrated for a whole week before that day). The annual ceremony begins with the charter being read in traditional costume outside the church, and the pubs where a drink of rum and milk is consumed. The procession includes a group of bodyguards for the charter reader.

(After opening the Fair. 1900)

Left: In 2004, the fair saw the 800th anniversary of the granting of the charter. Among the celebrations a competition was held for the best recipe for Rothwell Tarts, traditionally made for the occasion, with the basic ingredients of curd cheese and lemon. Here a group of halberdiers march down Bridge Street towards High Street. The photograph was taken from the balcony of the recently formed Rothwell Arts and Heritage Centre.

Below: Celebrating the Coronation of King Edward VII, Thursday 26 June 1902, at Gretton. Mrs Gibbon, a village benefactor, is presenting Coronation mugs to the village children in the garden of Gretton House.

Right: Celebrating the Coronation of George V, 11 June 1911, at Oundle. In addition to the intriguing activities listed here, there was orange bobbing, a decorated bicycle competition (with a first prize of 7s 6d), 'snapping the treacle buns' (probably a game where children tried to grab buns, which were tied to strings, with their teeth) and a baby show.

Below: Lord and Lady Brooke inside the village hall at Great Oakley, 12 May 1937, the occasion being the Coronation of George VI after his brother had abdicated in December of the previous year. The occasion was broadcast to the nation by royal command and here Lord Brooke can be seen seated by the radio tuning in, while his wife is dressed in finery for the occasion with two page boys holding the train of her gown, watched by some of the villagers.

G.   R.

CORONATION OF KING GEORGE V.

OUNDLE SPORTS.

Thursday, 22nd Day of June, 1911,

TO COMMENCE AT 2.15 P.M.

1. **Walking Race for Men over 60 years of age,** from Townley House to Town Hall. Prizes: First, value 3s. Second, 2s. ; Third, 1s.

   Rowland Clark, Benefield Road   Orlando Leayton, North Street
   William West, Church Lane

2. **Jumping Race in Sacks,** from New Street to Town Hall. Prizes: First, value 3s. ; Second, 2s. ; Third, 1s.

   Bertie Loakes, Station Road   Charles Fox, West Street
   Charles Fisher, Havelock Cottages   Percy Munds, Market Place
   Marcus Fox, junr., West Street

3. **Tug of War (Married v. Single).** Fifteen a side. Two captains to choose teams. Prize : 15s. Post entry.

4. **Find Your Clothes Race, for Young Men.** Waistcoats, coats and caps twisted together in heaps at given points. Competitors to dress and then return to winning post. Prizes: First, value 3s. ; Second, 2s. ; Third, 1s.

   Charles Fisher, Havelock Cottages   Bertie Loakes, Station Road
   Tom Sharpe, Havelock Cottages   Charlie Fox, West Street

5. **Three-legged Race.** Prizes: First, value 3s. ; Second, 2s. ; Third, 1s.

   Gladys Sawford, 3, Burnham Terrace,   Fred Marshall, North Street
       East Road   Arthur Williams, St. Osyth's Lane
   Ethel Fenton, Rock Road   Harry Sismore, North Street
   Bertie Loakes, Station Road   Edward Marshall, North Street
   Tom Sharpe, Havelock Cottages   Percy Munds, Market Place
   Charles Fisher, Havelock Cottages   Charles Fox, West Street
   Patrick Woodford, Drummingwell
       Yard

Celebrating the Coronation of George VI at Gretton, 1937. The village celebrated the event in a unique way by having its own king and queen – in the form of two ladies (Mrs J. Lattimer and Mrs Curtis respectively), and a specially decorated Coronation Coach, driven by Mr D. Wooton (left) and Mr B. Fursdon.

Celebrating the Coronation of Elizabeth II at Grafton Underwood, 2 June 1953. Five days earlier, Edmund Hilary and Sherpa Tenzing had reached the summit of Mount Everest, an historically great achievement at the time. Among the festivities in the village was a fancy dress competition, and it was perhaps fitting that the 'mountaineer' in the centre of the group was the winner.

Empire Day, Rowlett School, Corby village, May 1929. The page boy sitting on the far left is Bob Mears who later went on to run the Corby Photographic Society, and Queen Elizabeth I is Francis Dixon. Empire Day came into being in 1902 at the end of the Boer War, in recognition of the achievements of the British Empire and was celebrated annually, mainly by children.

Empire Day, Brigstock in the 1920s. Among those surrounding an imposing central 'Britannia' are costumed figures representing South Africa, India and the Far East.

On 12 November 1844, Queen Victoria passed through the Rockingham Forest area en route to a christening at Burghley House. Triumphal arches were erected, buildings festooned, and bell ringing, flag waving and cheers greeted the royal procession as it passed through each settlement. Her coach and horses entered Kettering (seen here) where the royal party stopped for refreshments and a change of horses at the White Hart. For a special treat, over 1,000 Sunday school children were given a grand tea to mark the occasion.

Rockingham Forest Discovery Day, 6 July 1996. This event was held to raise awareness of the Forest and its rich heritage. Here, a group of participants are standing with a guide under a boundary oak tree in Wakerley Woods.

A costumed event performed by children from the National School, Oundle, 1902. The 'king' standing at the centre of the back row is W. Ellis, whose sister is in the middle row (second left).

A Festival of Britain parade, Brigstock, 1951. This was one of several special events that took place during the village's Festival Week including a beauty pageant, baby show, tug o' war, and comic cricket match (where the result did not matter!). As well as marking the centenary of the Great Exhibition and celebrating post-war Britain, the object was to raise funds to cover a debt owing on the new village hall. For this parade, age was no barrier, and there were fifty-four entrants all participating in good humour.

Empire's Honour group, Kingscliffe in the 1920s. This was a costumed pageant that took place in the village during the First World War. Among those dressed in colourful costume in the yard of the Endowed School are (far left) Mr Love, who was headmaster of the school, and the Revd Orlebar, vicar of All Saints and St James.

Princess Margaret passing through Grafton Underwood, Summer 1956. The princess was on a private visit to nearby Boughton House, and villagers lined the streets for the occasion, among them this group of flag-waving children.

A Rockingham Forest perambulation, May 1995. Three inspired 'officials' take a break from inspecting and confirming a section of the old boundary of the Forest at the 370-year-old hollow ash in Fineshade Woods. Left to right: Peter Hill, Dan Keech and Chris Wade.

The opening of the first Co-op, High Street, Brigstock, 1926. The store, which was built on the site of a pub and farmhouse, provided a valuable service for the large village, and is still flourishing. Older villagers have fond memories of the store's earlier days, with everything being weighed out on scales, and the delicious smells from the hams being cooked at the rear of the shop.

MANOR OF

Wadenhoe.

The Game on this Manor is intended to be preserved,

And Notice is hereby given, that the Tenants and Gamekeeper are directed to lay Informations against all unqualified Persons and Poachers, who may be found attempting to take or destroy the Game; and all qualified Persons who shall be discovered sporting without having obtained leave, will be prosecuted as Trespassers.

"By order of the Lord of the Manor."

Wadenhoe, 16th August, 1819

Printed by T. Bell, Oundle.

Above: Members of Oundle Operatic Society, 1930s. From left to right, back row: Messrs Martin, Todd, Pywell and Elliott. Front row: Mrs Scott, Mrs Richards, Mrs Fellows and Miss Horne.

Left: Although Forest Law had long been defunct, poaching was still illegal, and widespread, but now rabbits and game had become the main quarry. Private landowners made it clear what the consequences would be for anyone caught: transportation was not an unknown occurrence for the convicted. This poster from Wadenhoe dating from 1819 was for the Ward–Hunt estate.

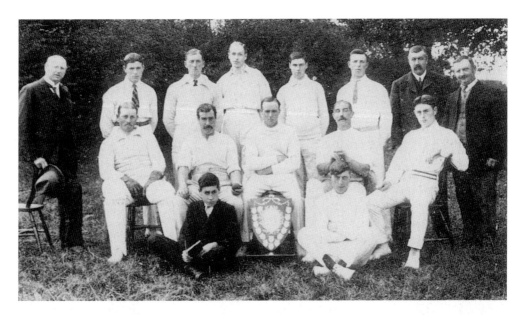

Great Oakley Cricket Team, displaying the 2nd Division Silver Challenge Shield of the Kettering and District Cricket League, 1913. This was the second time they had won the championship, the previous occasion being in 1896. From left to right, back row: Sir Arthur de Capell Brooke (president), Arthur Sherratt, Ken Northen, Charles Palmer, Sam Essam, William Tebbutt, William Cross (the gardener at Oakley Hall), Jonathan Tebbutt (the village vet). Middle row: Edward Northen, Tom Julian, Harold Bagshaw (captain), James Payne, Charles Sherratt. Front row: Norman Cross and Charles Marlow.

Brigstock Rovers Football Team, 1905/06. The team later changed its name to Brigstock St Peter's, and produced a future county star player, Jack Starsmore (one of five footballing brothers), who played for Desborough, and Kettering Town.

Rockingham Hill, 1929. A group of children from Cottingham Methodist Chapel are on their annual outing, or 'Grand Tour' of the area. Transportation was always by horse and cart, Rockingham providing two or three of these for the occasion. This particular group is being driven by Charles Liquorish. At the end of the excursion, the children always had a tea party at the chapel.

Hounds at Brigstock. The Woodland Pytchley Hunt was established in the village in 1873 by G.L. Watson. The annual Boxing Day Hunt soon became a tradition in the village, and an integral part of the Christmas season. The chase could cover up to thirty miles.

Nassington Brass Band, *c.* 1900. The musicians are standing opposite the Black Horse pub in Station Road. The houses behind the band have long since vanished. The band eventually ceased and some members were absorbed into the Yarwell and Nassington Britannia Band. The marching drum seen here was a prominent feature of both bands.

A group of Brigstock villagers pose with musical instruments at the rear of the Green Dragon pub, 1890. Among them are members of the Hector family.

Sack wrestling at Middleton village fête, 1950s. George 'Sketch' Patrick is seen here. The fête was held at the old village hall on the Ashley Road.

Cottingham Weslyan Brass Band, 1924. The band is marching up Middleton Hill, and is believed to be leading the Methodist church schoolchildren out of the village on their annual outing, the Round in the Wagons, to Rockingham and beyond.

four

The Forest at War

Above: A local group of the Royal Observer Corps at Deenethorpe Airfield prepare for a flight in 1945. The man standing on the extreme left is one-time local pub landlord and actor 'Fatty Moffat' whose claim to fame was appearing in British comedy films with Will Hay.

Left: When a German Dornier bomber plane was shot down just south of Weldon in February 1943, a mystery surrounded the discovery of five bodies in what was normally a four-man aircraft. It was believed the fifth member was a spy on a special mission. Names were later added to four of the five grave markers, two of which are seen above in Weldon churchyard. The fifth marker was never inscribed with a name.

Cottages and houses lining the narrow streets of Weldon were often scraped and gouged, as was the road surface, by tanks from a large tank base at Deene passing through the village. On 21 January 1941, however, considerable damage was done to a house in Church Street, when a US truck crashed into the wall of a house in Church Street, destroying part of the area around the doorway.

Brigstock Camp was originally set up and occupied as a Ministry of Labour Testing Centre in 1929 to alleviate unemployment in the realm. In August 1939, it was handed over to the Ministry of Defence who refurbished it as a militia training camp, adding new huts, a dining hall and cookhouse. It was used by US troops until the 1950s and later fell into a state of disrepair, as seen here.

The May Day procession at Great Oakley, 1944. The children are standing with their May garland at the front porch of Great Oakley Hall in anticipation of a treat. The May Queen is Jill Austin and the group contains some wartime evacuees from London living in the village at the time.

At the time of the second Boer War (1899-1901), there was demand for young men with riding and shooting skills, and the Forest area contributed its fair share of recruits, including Arthur Arnold of Deenethorpe, seen here in his uniform on his return to Deene Park in 1902.

Land Army girls at Brigstock. In May 1942, the first batch of girls, all from different backgrounds, arrived in the village and joined local girls in carrying out agricultural work within a nine-mile radius of the hostel which consisted of huts specially erected near the corner of Benefield Road and Back Lane.

Grafton Underwood was the one of the first British airfields put at the disposal of the US 8th Army Airforce. Bombing missions were flown from August 1942 to April 1945, during which time 159 aircraft were lost and an astounding 1,579 lost their lives. Here, a B17 Flying Fortress is flying parallel with the Thrapston–Oundle road (foreground), and the village of Titchmarsh can be seen under the wing.

Second World War evacuees at Grafton Underwood Airfield, 1944. Many children staying with local families had fond memories of the area, and this was one of the highlights. The US airmen loved all children and laid on entertainment and parties for them. This group is pictured on a jeep driven by a local Red Cross girl.

Kingscliffe Airfield was a small airfield for just two squadrons, using mainly Mustang fighters. It was described as 'one of the poorest airfields in England' and 'an abundance of mud'. This did not deter the men based on the site from carrying out their tasks and missions. Pilots frequently painted descriptive names, and the number of enemy aircraft they had downed, on the fuselage of their planes, as seen here.

Right: A group of US airmen pose at Kingscliffe Airfield, the base of the 20th Fighter Group, 1944. From left to right, top row: ? Lee, ? Pogue and ? Beschen. Bottom row: -?-, ? Schons.

Below: A first-aid crew at Kingscliffe Airfield, 1944. From left to right: Sgt. Calka, Capt. Paul 'Doc' Roberts, Staff Sgt. Eid, Corp. Graham.

The Imperials, a dance band, are playing one of their regular engagements at Kingscliffe Airfield. Strong links were formed by those at the airfield with the local community; the dances providing the opportunity for village girls to escape the austere climate of the war. In one magnanimous gesture, the airmen distributed oranges to the children of Kingscliffe and nearby Forest villages during an outbreak of rickets.

The first unit to be based at Kingscliffe Airfield was the 79th Fighter Squadron. A pilot demonstrates a particular manoeuvre of interest to the assembled crew, several of whom would later perish on combat missions. A total of 132 fighter planes from the base were lost during the war.

Members of Geddington Home Guard, 1941–42. From left to right, back row: C. Ayres, P. Carver, A. Chamberlain, -?-, -?-, A. Hopkins, W. Digby, -?-. Front row: -?-, G. Lane, -?-, F. Bepridge, F. Coles, W. Abbott, H. Hopkins.

VE Day at Deene Close in Corby, 8 May 1945. Celebrations took place all over the kingdom to mark the official end of the war, with streets festooned with flags and street parties. The children are, from left to right: Roger Hawkins, Jean Banon, Darren Charnly, -?-, Mary Anderson, Richard Charnly, Edward Charnly, Julie Hawkins, Barbara Trowman, Jean Sweeny, Betty Vale, Morean Anderson, Betty Banon, Jean Charnly, Mary McLine, Tommy Preston, Helen McCartney, Dianne Charnly.

A VE Day street party in Corby, 8 May 1945. The group enjoying themselves are residents of Clarke Road. The occasion was marked with street dancing, the music provided by an accordion, a piano and the radio. Despite wartime rationing, the community rallied together with the help of local shopkeepers and bakers, and the tables were filled with jellies, spam and cooked meats, and cakes with a marzipan substitute made from semolina.

Erection of the war memorial, Cottingham/Middleton, Remembrance Day, 1920. The event took place on Mill Road, near the boundary between the two villages, in front of where a modern school stands today.

Left: Mrs Stokes, wife of Dr Stokes of Weldon, sitting outside their home, Cheyne House.

Below: Nassington church choir, 1910. Members include the church 'organ blower', Joe Crowson (centre, second row), the vicar, the Revd Percival (to the right of the tall man in the centre of the back row), and next to him the village schoolmaster, Mr Hoare. The two ladies seated on the left are the vicar's wife, Mrs Percival (holding a copy of Handel's *Judas Maccabaeus*) and her housekeeper; the two ladies seated on the right are the organist Mrs Hoare and her daughter, Janet.

With its contasting landscape of fields, woods and waterways, the Forest area has always been excellent for horseriding. This photo, taken in the early 1900s, is believed to be of Lady Ethel Wickham of Cotterstock Hall.

This scene is unusual in that two horses in single file are being harnessed to pull the trap. It shows Annie Stokes of Weldon in the yard of her home, around 1925.

Jabez Rowell (1856-1924) came to Brigstock from Oundle and started a successful fellmongering business in the village which flourished for many years in the area. A deeply religious man and a zealous churchgoer, he expected both his family and his employees to go to three services each Sunday.

This photograph by Oakley Ireson shows his son (also named Oakley) with his wife and their beehives in the garden at the rear of their home in Station Road, Nassington, in the 1920s.

Copyholders' Annual Dinner, Middleton, early 1900s. The occasion took place at the rear of the Exeter Arms (no longer a hostelry) in Main Street. From left to right: George Binley (the landlord), Alf Bradshaw, J. Claypole, John Chamberlain, Harry Buswell, T. Curtis, C. Dexter, J. West, Sam Swingler, J. Sharman, William Aldwinckle, J.T. Spriggs, ? Spriggs, Christopher Robert Simpson, William Reynolds, Charles Bradshaw, ? Ingram.

The Revd John Poole Sandlands, vicar of Brigstock for forty-two years (1856-1915), had ideas which make sense to us today, but which were seen as unorthodox and nonsense by many of his contemporaries. He wrote pamphlets and books advocating a sensible diet with 'natural food', plenty of exercise, and abstention from smoking. A strict vegetarian and enthusiastic walker, his ideas attracted many people from far and wide, who came to him for advice on the treatment and cures of various ailments.

Bamford Spendlove of Warren Farm (later Manor Farm), Gretton, *c.* 1900. The Spendloves lived at nearby Deene in the late sixteenth century, and were later associated with Gretton from the 1820s, since when they have flourished until the present day.

Wilbarston, early 1900s. The man on the donkey, Mr Bell, is said to have used the animal for getting to his workplace in the Forest. The building in the background stands next to the entrance to the woodyard off Main Street.

Cottingham Scout troop, 1950s. The scoutmasters are Les Jackson and Mr H.V. Porter, headmaster of the village school.

Middleton, *c.* 1902. A group of villagers stand outside the old Red Lion. The landlord, George Bayes, and his wife, Ann, are pictured in the trap to the left, with relatives and members of the Vickers family. The hostelry has since been replaced by a newer building, which stands further back from the street.

In the 1920s Connie Woolston was reputed to have been the first woman in the county to ride a motorcycle. Here she is outside the old Great Oakley post office with her mother, Maria, standing in the doorway.

Dr Arthur Stokes of Weldon, *c.* 1920. Based at Cheyne House, the doctor's practice covered a wide area and he was a familiar figure with his pony and trap whenever he was called out to a neighbouring village. One of his passions was photography, and his camera was responsible for several high-quality images of local scenes and people.

Right: The Revd Wentworth Watson of Rockingham Castle. In 1900, he had inherited the castle from his childless older brother, George, and began to make important alterations to the interior including a restyling of the library. On his death, in July 1925, the castle passed for a short time to his nephew, and then to Commander Sir Michael Culme-Seymour.

Below: Children of Nassington School proudly display their shield as winners of the North Northamptonshire Music Festival, held in the Great Hall at Oundle School, 1921. They are with the tutor, Mrs Hewitt, who successfully coached them to success. The two girls holding the shield are Nora Kiddersley and Jannie Brown.

Wilbarston School, early 1900s. Lying at the foot of School Hill, it started life as a National School for ninety-six children in 1845, and is still flourishing, though mainly in an adjacent modern building.

Great Oakley School, 1907. The school, for thirty-five chidren, was built in 1867 by Sir William de Capell Brooke, and closed in 1957. Among those identified in the group are three Tebbutt sisters, a family associated with the village since the seventeenth century. The youngest sister, Elsie, second from the right in the front row, lived to be well over 100 years old. The teacher on the right, Mrs Green, was a no-nonsense person, who, unusually for the time, caused angry parents to confront her about an over-zealous tendency for punishment!

Cottingham cum Middleton School, early 1900s. This is the junior class pictured outside the school (built in 1871, originally for eighty-two children) in School Lane, Cottingham. Before this, children had gone to a school that had been built in 1856 in adjoining Middleton. Music was obviously a favourite subject. From left to right, back row are: Louie Botterill, ? Dunkley, Sam Claypole, Mabel Tansley, Elsie Bell, -?-, Louie Spriggs. Middle row: Edith Vickers, Jessie Binley, Tom Darnell, -?-, Spennie Reynolds, Fred Lines, Harry Fisher, Arthur Inchley, Harry Foster, Percy Chamberlain, Ida Beecroft, Thomas Beecroft (headmaster). Next row: Cissie Shrives, ? Read, Annie Bamford, Ethel Binley, Lily Chamberlain, Annie Spriggs, Irene Coles, Harry Beecroft. Front row: Jim Tansley, Sid Binley, Gordon Shrives, Neville Chamberlain, Dorothy Reynolds, Lily Bush. A newer purpose-built school at another site on the road to Bringhurst now serves both Cottingham and neighbouring Middleton.

Weldon School, *c.* 1898. This scene is unusual for a mixed village school in that it is all-female (though fee-paying private schools were usually of one gender). The school, which faces the village green, was one of the earliest to be built in the Forest area. It was opened in 1820, and extended in 1872 and 1891, but like so many others, is no longer in use.

A group of villagers standing at the well-head, Cottingham, early 1930s. The well stood on the corner of Corby Road and Rockingham Road, and was inscribed: Erected by the copyholders, 1854, William Thorpe, John Spriggs, Bailiffs. The site is now covered over by a grassy slope with a colourful village sign by local designer, Chris Owen.

six

Forest Places

Above: Kirby Hall, *c.* 1890. The Hall was built on the site of a former house in 1570-1575 by Sir Humphrey Stafford of Blatherwycke, on whose death it was sold to Sir Christopher Hatton, Chancellor to Elizabeth I, who added other features which necessitated the removal of the village of Kirby and its church.

Left: Queen Mary, wife of George V, on a visit to Kirby Hall, 1932. With her is the custodian, Mr J. Hawkes, who resided in part of the building.

This fine aerial view of Rockingham Castle and its grounds was taken around 1930 and shows the castle complex and part of its extensive grounds, the gardens of which cover over 5 hectares (12 acres). The circular feature on the extreme right is a rose garden enclosed within a yew hedge, which, like the other gardens, was developed during the Tudor and Stuart periods. The cross-like feature in the foreground is a terraced garden, to the left of which is a substantial double yew hedge. At the top right lies the colourfully named Tilting Ground, which was created out of the southern bailey of the original Norman castle. Out of view among the trees in the foreground, a 'natural' or wild garden, fashionable during the nineteenth century, was created in a ravine with exotic trees and shrubs, and a wishing well. Charles Dickens stayed at the castle on at least five occasions and is believed to have been inspired by the grounds and local landscape for Chesney Wold in his novel, *Bleak House*. He is said to have seen the ghost of Lady Deadlock, who supposedly haunted the grounds, flitting about the yew hedge. During his visits he wrote and performed playlets for the family of Richard and Lavinia Watson and their guests in the Long Gallery. He also dedicated his novel *David Copperfield* to his hosts.

Rockingham Castle, *c.* 1930. A motte and bailey castle from the time of William I was replaced by a stone structure, which, under Edward I, was extensively modernised and fortified, including the addition of two great round towers on the gatehouse seen here. King John was a regular visitor in the early thirteenth century, leaving behind one of his possessions: an iron chest. The building and grounds eventually passed (on a lease) in 1530 to a local landowner, Edward Watson who rebuilt it into a fine residence, and in 1619 it was bought outright by Sir Lewis Watson.

Southwick Hall, *c.* 1960. This part fourteenth-century building is one of the oldest in the county, and has been owned by three successive families: the Knyvetts, Lynns and Caprons. This view from the west shows the predominantly eighteenth-century exterior (left and centre) while to the right is the oldest (medieval) part of the Hall which houses the Priest's Room and a fine vaulted undercroft.

Rushton Hall, *c.* 1930. The Hall was begun around 1508 by John Tresham and subsequently enlarged by his great grandson, Sir Thomas, and later by members of the Cockayne family, who acquired the estate from the Crown after its confiscation from Francis Tresham, who had been involved in the Gunpowder Plot. In the eighteenth century, some of the buildings in the grounds, together with the 'village' of Rushton St Peter and the church (which stood on the green area to the right), were demolished.

Fermyn Woods Hall, *c.* 1928. Lying on the Brigstock–Benefield road, the original building began in the fourteenth century as a small lodge for Forest officials. It then passed into the hands of private owners who extended the building to its present size. The seventeenth-century gateway fronting the house is engraved with the Tresham family crest, and came originally from nearby Lyveden Old Bield.

The original main entrance to the grounds of Apethorpe Hall, 1920. Virtually everything in this scene is unrecognisable today; the driveway is now grassed over, the gateway bricked in and the iron railings moved to another location beyond the manor house, the building (with four dormer windows) in the distance. The ornate house in the foreground, and the building with the wide chimney behind the gateway no longer exist. Access to the Hall grounds today is via a turning off the Kingscliffe road.

Apethorpe Hall. The original building was begun in the late fifteenth century and passed through the hands of Sir Guy Wolston, Sir Walter Mildmay (Chancellor of the Exchequer under Elizabeth I), and in the seventeenth century Sir Francis Fane (Earl of Westmorland) and his family until 1904. In 2002, the building, which had been deteriorating after a long period of being unoccupied by new owners since 1978, was taken over by English Heritage and is currently undergoing restoration.

Right: The unique Triangular Lodge at Rushton, *c.* 1890. Built by Thomas Tresham betwen 1593 and 1597, ostensibly as an expression of his Catholic faith in a zealously Protestant era, it symbolises the Holy Trinity, with everything in sets or multiples of three. Known 'officially' at the time as the Warryner's Lodge – for the use of the estate rabbit catcher – it was later linked to the Gunpowder Plot as a supposed meeting place for Tresham's son, Francis, and the conspirators.

Below: Lyveden New Bield was built by Thomas Tresham as yet another symbol of his religious fanaticism. Built to a cruciform plan, it symbolised the Passion, with a frieze around the outside depicting this. It was built in 1604-05 and left unfinished on his death, without a roof. Today it is in the care of the National Trust who have also restored the adjoining water gardens, and replanted a Tudor orchard.

Above: The church of St Mary the Virgin and All Saints, Kingscliffe, around 1948 seen from the corner of Bridge Street. It is unusual (like Duddington) in having a central tower, and its irregular plan indicative of a pre-Conquest building. The rectangular structure behind the railings in the churchyard is the tomb (in the form of a writing desk) of William Law, the village benefactor and theologian, who, with his acolyte, Elizabeth Hutcheson, was responsible for the provision of almshouses and schools on the road to Apethorpe.

Left: The church of Nassington, under repair in 1905 after lightning struck the steeple in May that year. Part of the Manor House can be seen on the extreme right.

An aerial view of Great Oakley Hall and the church of St Michael. This was taken from a light aircraft by village cine-enthusiast, Peter Bagshaw, in 1961, shortly after the church was re-roofed. Note the unusual low pitch of the roof and the distinctively shaped yew trees in the foreground.

Drayton Manor, near Lowick, *c.* 1930. Once connected with a branch of the de Vere family, members of whom took the name 'de Drayton', it was fortified in 1328 and enlarged over the following centuries. Parts of the original building still survive, including a solar undercroft and a wall of the south front.

In 1778, the church of St Peter, at Lilford was demolished for estate development. Parts of the structure were numbered and transported by cart to nearby woods, The Linches, at Thorpe Achurch, where the masonry was reconstructed in an isolated location among the trees overlooking the river Nene.

The church of St Andrew, Brigstock, *c.* 1948, from the grounds of the Manor House. The fine semi-circular Saxon stair turret (similar to that at Brixworth) can be seen adjoining the tower with its fine broach spire.

The stocks and whipping post at Gretton, early 1900s. These still exist today (though they are no longer in use) on the green facing the church. The Gretton Stores can be seen to the right, and the building to the left later became a butcher's shop. Both are now private homes.

The Rose and Crown, Main Street, Aldwincle, *c.* 1910. At one time the village had as many as seven public houses and beer retailers, but like twelve other Forest villages is now 'dry'. The building still survives, used now as a residence, as do those of the Castle (now Tavern Cottage) and Red Lion, both of which were tied to the brewers, Tebbutt, who operated from the neighbouring village of Sudborough, where the Round House was another of their outlets.

The Three Horseshoes, Nassington, *c.* 1899. Standing from left to right are: Sam Kirman, the publican (and train driver), his wife, and the local 'bobby' P.C. Brown. Over the years, the Forest has lost at least 220 public houses, of which this is another casualty, though the distinct building still survives, on Apethorpe Road.

The Sea Horse, Deene, *c.* 1920. This fine old inn, formerly known as the White Hart, took its name from the crest of the Brudenell family of Deene Park, lords of the manor since 1514. This impressive building (part sixteenth century) accommodated many visitors as well as locals, but has long ceased to function as a hostelry. The pony and trap belonged to Dr Arthur Stokes of Weldon who took this photograph while passing through.

The former Royal George, Wood Street, Geddington, 1960, shortly after its conversion to a private house. Despite the loss of this hostelry and three others, the Royal Oak, the Angel, and the Duke's Arms, the village still has three public houses.

Stocks Hill, Duddington, *c.* 1896. Facing a triangular green, is the Crown, with its propietor, Thomas Sanders (whose other occupations were 'overseer' and farmer) and his staff standing outside. It has since been demolished. Its nearby companion, the Windmill, is now a private house, leaving the Royal Oak as the only survivor of the three hostelries that formerly served the village. The long building to the left is Stocks Hill House, which has sixteenth-century features, and has since been tastefully restored. The small adjoining building functioned at this time as a shop. The church of St Mary, with its unusual central tower, lies in the distance.

The Anchor Inn, St Osyth's Lane, Oundle, 1930s. This was one of the town's ancient hostelries, and was rebuilt in 1637. Affectionately known as the Duck's Nest, it was eventually demolished, and a supermarket now stands on its site.

The Woolpack, Cranford, *c.* 1904. Once one of the most attractive public houses in the Forest area, it closed in 1999 and like so many other redundant hostelries, is now a private residence. It was one of three pubs in the village, with the Stag, and the Red Lion, the latter being the only survivor today. The village is split into two parishes, Cranford St Andrew, and Cranford St John, which are separated from each other by a stream.

The Angel, High Street, Brigstock, c. 1910. This was one of the first of Brigstock's one-time thirteen hostelries to close. It subsequently became a butcher's shop for many years, and is now a private house.

The Crown Inn, Cottingham, early 1900s. The landlord, Alfred Buswell, and his daughters are standing outside the hostelry, which stood on the corner of Rockingham Road and School Lane, close to the Spread Eagle. It has long since disappeared.

Gretton, early 1900s. The thatched building forms the centre of three cottages which are known as Seven Steeples. The woman on the right is Ellen Wormall (*née* Coles, born around 1876). Note the potato clamp in the foreground, and the slightly out of place corrugated iron sheeting covering the thatch. The nuts of the overhanging walnut tree were collected and sold in quantities of fifteen or twenty for a penny. When the three cottages were offered for sale, the tree was sold separately for its wood, fetching the sum of £150.

Flooding in Queen Street, Geddington, 27 August 1912. Of all the villages in Rockingham Forest, perhaps Geddington is the most vulnerable to flooding. The river Ise frequently bursts its banks, often dramatically, the last occasions being Easter 1998, described as 'the biggest disaster since the war', which was followed a few months later by more devastating floods on 28 October (such was the turmoil that even ducks took to higher ground, preferring to sit on the roofs of cottages). The magnificent medieval bridge (partly rebuilt in the eighteenth century) with its cutwaters and three pedestrian refuges can be seen in the background, beyond which lies Bridge Street, and the church of St Mary Magdalene. The water has risen above the ford to the left of the bridge so that the streets have become an extension of the river. One of the village wells (with a capstone) can be seen on the left in front of the Congregational church (out of view). The shop on the left selling mineral waters and tea is now a private house. The seventeenth-century thatched building on the right was one of the village's bakehouses. Note the lantern thoughtfully placed in the water behind the cart for navigation through the flood at night.

Opposite below: Little Oakley, January 1926. The left-hand approach to the hump-backed stone bridge is now hedged in. The bridge itself has since disappeared and been replaced with a concrete structure, and the surface levelled, though the remains of the old washbrook for horse and cart still lie at each end of the bridge. Apart from these changes, the scene is much the same today .

Flooding at Geddington, 2 July 1958, taken from the steps of the Eleanor Cross. The use of a boat to get around, with oarsmen in naval uniform, seems very appropiate! Here, Pam Giles of the WMC is the lucky passenger.

Flooding at Weekley and Warkton, 27 August 1912. Another of the villages on the river Ise badly hit by the 1912 floods. The long thatched house (demolished in 1921) was divided into three cottages (Folly Cottages), occupied at the time by the Symonds, Allsops and Colemans. The end house sold soft drinks, and the sign in the window is advertising 'Cook's Mineral Waters'. The toilets to these houses were reached via a bridle path leading into Weekley village.

Top Lodge, Rockingham, *c.* 1930. Lying near the crest of Rockingham Hill, this was one of two lodges standing at entrances to the castle and its grounds. The building dates from the mid-nineteenth century and has the coat of arms of the Watson family on the front wall. This side of the Rockingham–Kettering road was lined with a great number of trees at the time.

The War Memorial Chapel and St Anthony House, Oundle, *c.* 1952. These are two of the many substantial buildings belonging to Oundle School. The chapel was consecrated in 1923 and opened in 1926. St Anthony House, standing on the opposite side of Milton Road, was opened in January 1928 as accommodation for pupils at the school.

Left: Gretton, early 1930s. Mrs Alice Spence with her daughters Nellie and Nancy are standing outside their home, Geneva Cottage, on Harringworth Road.

Below: Mrs Louise Love standing at the gate of her cottage, Main Street, Lower Glapthorn, late 1930s. A modern bungalow now stands on the site opposite the village hall. Glapthorn is divided into two parts, Upper and Lower, which are separated by a brook.

Brigstock Market Cross, *c.* 1902. The original weekly markets, which no longer take place, were granted during the reigns of Edward IV in 1466 (Saturdays) and James I in 1604 (Thursdays). The fine Market Cross is inscribed on its sides with the initials of four queens, together with the dates of the inscriptions, beginning with: Elizabeth I (ER 1586), Anne (AR 1705), Victoria (VR 1887) and finally, Elizabeth II (ER 1953). The building behind the cross was the workshop and home of A. Bird, boot and shoe maker.

North Bridge, Oundle, *c.* 1929. Supposedly the longest bridge on the Nene, along with those at Thrapston and Wansford, the present eleven-arched structure dates from 1912-14, when it was rebuilt and widened after floods had damaged the sixteenth-century bridge. It is one of three bridges in the town, the others being South Bridge on the Barnwell road, and Warren Bridge on the Stoke Doyle road.

Vicarage Cottage, Gretton, 1946. This is one of many thatched buildings that once graced the village and have now been demolished (sixteen since the Second World War). It stood beside a track leading to the Old Vicarage, and the rear of the church.

The village grocery store in Main Street, Brigstock, *c.* 1910. It was run at the time by M. Ross and is still trading today, albeit under a different name.

A rare survival of a medieval cross marking the boundary between Blatherwycke and Kingscliffe. Made of local limestone, its head is engraved on both sides with a cross within a circle.

The Bocase Stone, near Brigstock, *c.* 1898. Various fanciful theories have been given for the origin and meaning of the name, ranging from the name of a hunt leader (Brocas) to a place for archery practice (bow case), but its most likely derivation is from Norman French *bocage* – a field on the edge of a wood. The site probably acted as a communal meeting point of some kind, the stone replacing (and commemorating) an oak tree which had formerly stood there for the purpose.

The late sixteenth-century dovecote at Newton. With the redundant church of St Faith nearby, this is all that remains of the village of Little Newton and the manor house (demolished 1722). There are nesting boxes for 2,000 birds and one of the two low entrances has a substantial wooden door. A plaque is engraved, 'Maurice Tresham', a member of that illustrious county family.

Conegar Farm, Woodnewton. This 'chocolate box' view shows the former watermill and eighteenth-century millhouse spanning the Willow Brook.

Rockingham village, *c.* 1955. Little has changed in the village since reconstruction began after the Civil War when Parliamentary troops destroyed many of its buildings including the almshouses and the church. Much of the village had stood outside the castle walls, and was consequently resited along the main road, as seen here.

The Pond at Yarwell, *c.* 1930. It was situated at the village crossroads, on the corner of the road to Old Sulehay. It was later filled in, grassed over and is the site today of a colourful modern village sign.

The ford at Geddington, looking towards Bridge Street, *c.* 1910. The thirteenth-century bridge with its three cutwaters and pedestrian refuges, was partially rebuilt in 1784. Incredibly, this was a major route through the realm until 1925, when a bypass was built to take traffic away from the village.

Grafton Underwood, *c.* 1910. The group are standing by one of four small eighteenth-century bridges spanning Alledge Brook which runs the length of the village. It is renowned for its colonies of ducks which like to congregate in the street and a road sign alerting motorists to slow down can be seen in the vicinity today.

Church Street, Nassington, looking towards the church, 1950. The building on the far left is the Prebendal Manor House, the oldest continuously inhabited house in Northamptonshire. It dates partly from the thirteenth century, when the village was chosen as the base for a prebendary (member of the cathedral chapter) of the Lincoln Diocese, and the house was subsequently built on the site of an earlier timber building. The barn (with historical displays) and gardens are open to the public today as the Prebendal Manor Medieval Centre.

Warkton, winter 1932. The avenue of elm trees are remnants of a vast area of woodland planted around the Boughton House estates from 1708 by John Montagu. On completion, the total aggregate length was estimated at an incredible seventy miles. Subsequent felling and natural causes have depleted many of the avenues of elm, beech and lime, though impressive stretches can still be seen in the Forest area.

Left: The Apollo Belvedere statue, Blatherwycke, stands in splendid isolation on a slope overlooking the site of its former home, Blatherwycke Hall, which was demolished in 1948. The statue was consequently removed from the gardens of the Hall to its present position where it is currently inaccessible to the public.

Below: Duddington, *c.* 1929. This fine old bridge over the river Welland was repaired and widened in 1919. On the bridge is a post marking the boundary with Tixover in Rutland. In the background are the part seventeenth-century former watermill, and the church of St Mary.

Rushton, *c*. 1925. The shepherd is walking his sheep along Station Road from the junction with Desborough Road, towards the church of All Saints, with part of the cricket ground just visible on the right. Such a task would be impossible to carry out today, with a steady flow of traffic passing through the village.

Corby Road, Cottingham, looking towards The Cross and School Lane, *c*. 1910. Part of the Wesleyan Chapel can be seen on the left. This section of the street was the main 'shopping area' of the village, with a bakehouse (which at one time acted in a dual role as a fish and chip shop), and a butcher's shop on the left (now Greystones). A smithy operated on the opposite side of the road. The buildings to the immediate right, and those at the far end of the street, have since been demolished.

Middleton, *c.* 1930, looking down Main Street towards the boundary with Cottingham. The sign of the Exeter Arms (no longer a hostelry) can be seen further along the road on the right. Before this is the Congregational church (now a private home). The large eighteenth-century building on the left is known today as Cannam House. Constructed of limestone, it makes a striking contrast with the golden-coloured ironstone of most of the village's buildings.

Water Lane, Cottingham, *c.* 1920. The little boy with the scooter on the right is Bernard Beadsworth. The thoroughfare is well named; abounding in springs which tend to flood the surface. Both the village and neighbouring Middleton have several surviving pumps and other vestiges from the days before mains water was supplied to homes. The upper path to the left leads to and from the church, and a car in the background stands at the gateway to the vicarage.

Little Oakley, *c.* 1930. The village has retained an air of tranquillity and little change over the years, with few new homes being built and the formation of a close-knit community. The now-redundant thirteenth-century church of St Peter has some unusual internal features including the recumbent effigy of a medieval forester clutching an arrow, and a wall memorial depicting horned figures. The manor house, now Manor Farm, is out of view to the left of the church.

Grafton Underwood, June 1928. One of the best preserved villages in the Forest (it is a designated conservation area), it has remained virtually intact, with most of its thatched buildings still lining the street today.

Left: The medieval gateway to the former New Inn, Fotheringhay. Coats of arms of the York and other noble families decorate the façade. Like the Old Inn (see top, page 12), it accommodated the overflow of guests at the castle. Today it is known as Garden Farm.

Below: The church of St Mary the Virgin at Nassington, as seen from Church Street, *c.* 1950. The tower has a fifteenth-century octagonal belfry and crocketed spire. The church was restored in 1885, and there are fine remnants of medieval wall paintings to be seen above the chancel arch and in the nave.

The Church, Nassington

Ashley Road, near the junction of the Desborough and Harborough roads, Stoke Albany, *c.* 1900. The girls are standing on part of a small area of grassland, adjoining what is now Green Lane.

Harborough Road, Stoke Albany, early 1900s. The hostelry sign in the distance is that of the White Horse on Desborough Road which still flourishes today. The White Hart Inn on the left was run at the time by Emmanuel Lee, but has since been demolished.

The church of All Saints, Wilbarston with its thirteenth-century broach spire as seen from Stoke Road, *c.* 1930. In the vicinity are an interesting group of features including former medieval fishponds, watermill, clapper bridge and ruined dovecote.

The bottom end of Stoke Albany, *c.* 1910. The boys are standing on the original village green, with the old school (built in 1871 and now the village hall), and the church of St Botolph in the background.

Above: The old village almshouse, Todds Hill, Duddington. The accommodation for the poor was originally in the two adjoining seventeenth-century cottages which were converted for the purpose in 1775.

Right: A typical old Forest cottage rear garden, Woodnewton, *c.* 1898. Such a peaceful, idyllic view has not completely vanished today, though stock features like a wooden ladder, wire hen coop, and horseshoe are no longer part and parcel of everyday life. The bicycle wheel hanging on the wall reflects the then increasingly popular pastime of cycling.

Other local titles published by Tempus

The Folklore of Northamptonshire

PETER HILL

Northamptonshire – Rose of the Shires – is a place of contrasts. Especially rich in traditions, dialect and vocabulary, legends, and wondrous stories that have been handed down through the ages, the character of Northamptonshire and its people is firmly rooted in its folklore. This fascinating illustrated study of folklore rediscovers those traditions and the beliefs, stories, maxims and superstitions of daily life, as well as music and verse, dance and song.

0-7524-3522-1

Around Oundle and Thrapston

PETER HILL

This fascinating collection of photographs provides a unique history of Oundle, a gateway town to Rockingham Forest in East Northamptonshire, and Thrapston, as well as other less well-documented villages in the area.

0 7524 0749 X

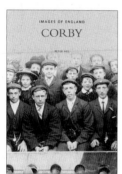

Corby

PETER HILL

Including many early images of the original village, now a shadow of its former self and with few of its original buildings still standing, this book provides an insight into the community that existed before the industry came.

0 7524 0723 6

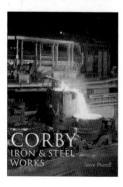

Corby Iron and Steel Works

STEVE PURCELL

Since Corby became the site of a new iron, steel and tube works in 1993, the village of 1,500 has grown into a new town of 60,000. Many of the families that arrived came from north of the border and Corby became known as 'Little Scotland'.

0 7524 2769 5

If you are interested in purchasing other books published by Tempus, or in case you have difficulty finding any Tempus books in your local bookshop, you can also place orders directly through our website

www.tempus-publishing.com